SAVORING THE JOYS

EMBRACING THE HARDSHIPS

225 Reflections for a Life Well Lived

Stoic, Philosophic & Timeless Wisdom

Curated by R. Brad Lebo, Ph.D.

ISBN 979-8-9850479-4-3

Printed on demand by IngramSpark.

Cover: case laminate, matte finish, 5 × 8 inches.

A note on quotations

All quotations in this journal are drawn from authors whose works are in the public domain, attributed in good faith based on scholarly consensus. A small number of attributions are traditional or disputed; these are noted where relevant.

Contents

A Note on This Collection

The quotes gathered here were drawn from one guiding question: what does it mean to live well?

All 225 voices belong to the public domain — philosophers, poets, sages, and storytellers who shaped the way human beings understand suffering, joy, connection, and freedom. From Marcus Aurelius writing by lamplight in a Roman military tent, to Rumi composing ecstatic verse in 13th-century Anatolia, to Thoreau surveying the pond at Walden — these words survived because they were true.

The seven themes are not meant as walls. A quote on acceptance may also be a quote on love. A quote on simplicity may also be a map back to yourself. Let them move freely.

"To find peace, savor the joys of life and embrace the hardships."

This journal is yours. Write honestly.

— R. Brad Lebo, Ph.D.

I · Acceptance & Letting Go

The first step toward peace is to release what was never ours to control.

"We suffer more in imagination than in reality."

— Seneca · 4 BC–65 AD

"We suffer more in imagination than in reality."

"It is not that I have little time, but that I waste much of what I have."

— Seneca · 4 BC–65 AD

"Seek not that the things which happen should happen as you wish; but wish the things which happen to be as they are, and you will have a tranquil flow of life."

— Epictetus · 50–135 AD

"No man ever steps in the same river twice, for it is not the same river and he is not the same man."

— Heraclitus · 535–475 BC

"Be content with what you have; rejoice in the way things are. When you realize there is nothing lacking, the whole world belongs to you."

— Lao Tzu · 6th century BC

"You must live in the present, launch yourself on every wave, find your eternity in each moment."

— Henry David Thoreau · 1817–1862

"Wear gratitude like a cloak, and it will feed every corner of your life."

— Rumi · 1207–1273

"Three things cannot be long hidden: the sun, the moon, and the truth."

— The Buddha · 563–483 BC

"Peace comes from within. Do not seek it without."

— The Buddha · 563–483 BC

"The wound is the place where the Light enters you."

— Rumi · 1207–1273

"Let us prepare our minds as if we had come to the very end of life. Let us postpone nothing."

— Seneca · 4 BC–65 AD

"*Begin at once to live, and count each separate day as a separate life.*"

— Seneca · 4 BC–65 AD

"Finish each day and be done with it. You have done what you could."

— Ralph Waldo Emerson · 1803–1882

> *"Freedom is secured not by the fulfilling of one's desires, but by the removal of desire."*
>
> — Epictetus · 50–135 AD

"Life is a series of natural and spontaneous changes. Don't resist them; that only creates sorrow."

— Lao Tzu · 6th century BC

"Change is the only constant in life."

— Heraclitus · 535–475 BC

"You only lose what you cling to."

— The Buddha · 563–483 BC

"Accept the things to which fate binds you, and love the people with whom fate brings you together, and do so with all your heart."

— Marcus Aurelius · 121–180 AD

"The greatest weapon against stress is our ability to choose one thought over another."

— William James · 1842–1910

"Out beyond ideas of wrongdoing and rightdoing, there is a field. I'll meet you there."

— Rumi · 1207–1273

"Loss is nothing else but change, and change is Nature's delight."

— Marcus Aurelius · 121–180 AD

"All of humanity's problems stem from man's inability to sit quietly in a room alone."

— Blaise Pascal · 1623–1662

"For every minute you are angry you lose sixty seconds of happiness."

— Ralph Waldo Emerson · 1803–1882

"*Never let the future disturb you. You will meet it, if you have to, with the same weapons of reason which today arm you against the present.*"

— Marcus Aurelius · 121–180 AD

*"Do not dwell in the past, do not dream of the future,
concentrate the mind on the present moment."*

— The Buddha · 563–483 BC

"Make the best use of what is in your power, and take the rest as it happens."

— Epictetus · 50–135 AD

*"Yesterday I was clever, so I wanted to change the world.
Today I am wise, so I am changing myself."*

— Rumi · 1207–1273

"Set your life on fire. Seek those who fan your flames."

— Rumi · 1207–1273

"Set your life on fire. Seek those who fan your flames."

"Wealth consists not in having great possessions, but in having few wants."

— Epictetus · 50–135 AD

II · The Present Moment & Savoring Life

Each day is a complete life. Receive it as such.

"To be able to look back upon one's life in satisfaction is to live twice."

— Kahlil Gibran · 1883–1931

"Beauty is not in the face; beauty is a light in the heart."

— Kahlil Gibran · 1883–1931

"What lies behind us and what lies before us are tiny matters compared to what lies within us."

— Ralph Waldo Emerson · 1803–1882

"The whole future lies in uncertainty: live immediately."

— Seneca · 4 BC–65 AD

"Nothing is worth more than this day."

— Johann Wolfgang von Goethe · 1749–1832

"Go confidently in the direction of your dreams. Live the life you have imagined."

— Henry David Thoreau · 1817–1862

"Nature does not hurry, yet everything is accomplished."

— Lao Tzu · 6th century BC

"Knowing is not enough; we must apply. Willing is not enough; we must do."

— Johann Wolfgang von Goethe · 1749–1832

"Very little is needed to make a happy life; it is all within yourself, in your way of thinking."

— Marcus Aurelius · 121–180 AD

"I have learned silence from the talkative, toleration from the intolerant, and kindness from the unkind."

— Kahlil Gibran · 1883–1931

"Respond to every call that excites your spirit."

— Rumi · 1207–1273

"In the sweetness of friendship let there be laughter and sharing of pleasures."

— Kahlil Gibran · 1883–1931

*"Do not go where the path may lead; go instead where there
is no path and leave a trail."*

— Ralph Waldo Emerson · 1803–1882

"The great use of life is to spend it for something that will outlast it."

— William James · 1842–1910

"Live in the sunshine, swim the sea, drink the wild air."

— Ralph Waldo Emerson · 1803–1882

"Knowing others is wisdom; knowing yourself is enlightenment."

— Lao Tzu · 6th century BC

"Beauty is truth, truth beauty — that is all ye know on earth, and all ye need to know."

— John Keats · 1795–1821

"You give but little when you give of your possessions. It is when you give of yourself that you truly give."

— Kahlil Gibran · 1883–1931

"When you arise in the morning, think of what a precious privilege it is to be alive — to breathe, to think, to enjoy, to love."

— Marcus Aurelius · 121–180 AD

"While we are postponing, life speeds by."

— Seneca · 4 BC–65 AD

"True happiness is to enjoy the present, without anxious dependence upon the future."

— Seneca · 4 BC–65 AD

"Stop acting so small. You are the universe in ecstatic motion."

— Rumi · 1207–1273

"Simplicity, patience, compassion. These three are your greatest treasures."

— Lao Tzu · 6th century BC

III · Resilience & Embracing Hardship

The oak grows strong in contrary winds.

"Most powerful is he who has himself in his own power."

— Seneca · 4 BC–65 AD

"Fire is the test of gold; adversity, of strong men."

— Seneca · 4 BC–65 AD

"It is not death that a man should fear, but he should fear never beginning to live."

— Marcus Aurelius · 121–180 AD

"*The quieter you become, the more you are able to hear.*"

— Rumi · 1207–1273

"When you do things from your soul, you feel a river moving in you, a joy."

— Rumi · 1207–1273

"The life given us by nature is short; but the memory of a well-spent life is eternal."

— Cicero · 106–43 BC

"What we plant in the soil of contemplation, we shall reap in the harvest of action."

— Meister Eckhart · 1260–1328

"A wise man will make more opportunities than he finds."

—— Francis Bacon · 1561–1626

"Know how to listen, and you will profit even from those who talk badly."

— Plutarch · 46–119 AD

"We are what we repeatedly do. Excellence, then, is not an act but a habit."

— Aristotle · 384–322 BC

"The mind is not a vessel to be filled, but a fire to be kindled."

— Plutarch · 46–119 AD

"Pleasure in the job puts perfection in the work."

— Aristotle · 384–322 BC

"The roots of education are bitter, but the fruit is sweet."

— Aristotle · 384–322 BC

"The man who moves a mountain begins by carrying away small stones."

— Confucius · 551–479 BC

"Character is destiny."

— Heraclitus · 535–475 BC

"There is only one way to happiness, and that is to cease worrying about things which are beyond the power of our will."

— Epictetus · 50–135 AD

"When it is obvious that the goals cannot be reached, don't adjust the goals; adjust the action steps."

— Confucius · 551–479 BC

"It does not matter how slowly you go as long as you do not stop."

— Confucius · 551–479 BC

"The remedy for wrongs is to forget them."

— Publilius Syrus · 1st century BC

"Luck is what happens when preparation meets opportunity."

— Seneca · 4 BC–65 AD

"Our greatest glory is not in never falling, but in rising every time we fall."

— Confucius · 551–479 BC

"If one oversteps the bounds of moderation, the greatest pleasures cease to please."

— Epictetus · 50–135 AD

"It is not because things are difficult that we do not dare; it is because we do not dare that things are difficult."

— Seneca · 4 BC–65 AD

"He who has a why to live can bear almost any how."

— Friedrich Nietzsche · 1844–1900

"No man is free who is not master of himself."

— Epictetus · 50–135 AD

"To make no mistakes is not in the power of man; but from their errors and mistakes the wise and good learn wisdom for the future."

—— Plutarch · 46–119 AD

"Any man can make mistakes, but only an idiot persists in his error."

— Cicero · 106–43 BC

"Difficulties are things that show a person what they are."

— Epictetus · 50–135 AD

"Happiness depends upon ourselves."

— Aristotle · 384–322 BC

"It is not what happens to you, but how you react to it that matters."

— Epictetus · 50–135 AD

IV · Virtue, Character & Living Well

Character is not what you claim. It is what you do when no one is watching.

"Character is higher than intellect."

— Ralph Waldo Emerson · 1803–1882

"In all things of nature there is something of the marvelous."

— Aristotle · 384–322 BC

"Lend yourself to others, but give yourself to yourself."

"To find yourself, think for yourself."

— Socrates · 470–399 BC

"Gratitude is not only the greatest of virtues, but the parent of all others."

— Cicero · 106–43 BC

"The first and greatest victory is to conquer yourself; to be conquered by yourself is of all things most shameful."

— Plato · 428–348 BC

"Waste no more time arguing about what a good man should be. Be one."

— Marcus Aurelius · 121–180 AD

"What you do speaks so loudly that I cannot hear what you say."

— Ralph Waldo Emerson · 1803–1882

"The happiness of your life depends upon the quality of your thoughts."

— Marcus Aurelius · 121–180 AD

"The measure of a man is what he does with power."

— Plato · 428–348 BC

"Character is like a tree and reputation like a shadow. The shadow is what we think of it; the tree is the real thing."

— Abraham Lincoln · 1809–1865

"It's never too late to be what you might have been."

— George Eliot · 1819–1880

"A hero is no braver than an ordinary man, but he is brave five minutes longer."

— Ralph Waldo Emerson · 1803–1882

"Most folks are about as happy as they make up their minds to be."

— Abraham Lincoln · 1809–1865

"It is the mark of an educated mind to be able to entertain a thought without accepting it."

— Aristotle · 384–322 BC

"To be yourself in a world that is constantly trying to make you something else is the greatest accomplishment."

— Ralph Waldo Emerson · 1803–1882

"What do we live for, if not to make life less difficult for each other?"

— George Eliot · 1819–1880

"An investment in knowledge pays the best interest."

— Benjamin Franklin · 1706–1790

"An investment in knowledge pays the best interest."

— Benjamin Franklin · 1706–1790

"*Good people do not need laws to tell them to act responsibly, while bad people will find a way around the laws.*"

— Plato · 428–348 BC

"The only true wisdom is in knowing you know nothing."

— Socrates · 470–399 BC

"*This above all: to thine own self be true.*"

— William Shakespeare · 1564–1616

"Happiness is the meaning and the purpose of life, the whole aim and end of human existence."

— Aristotle · 384–322 BC

"The higher we are placed, the more humbly we should walk."

— Cicero · 106–43 BC

"The best revenge is to be unlike him who performed the injury."

— Marcus Aurelius · 121–180 AD

"Be as you wish to seem."

— Socrates · 470–399 BC

"Whatever you are, be a good one."

— Abraham Lincoln · 1809–1865

V · Relationships, Love & Connection

We are knit together by invisible threads — gratitude, kindness, and the courage to be seen.

"It isn't what we say or think that defines us, but what we do."

— Jane Austen · 1775–1817

"Let there be spaces in your togetherness, and let the winds of the heavens dance between you."

— Kahlil Gibran · 1883–1931

"And ever has it been known that love knows not its own depth until the hour of separation."

— Kahlil Gibran · 1883–1931

"Your task is not to seek for love, but merely to seek and find all the barriers within yourself that you have built against it."

— Rumi · 1207–1273

"He whom love touches not walks in darkness."

— Plato · 428–348 BC

"Wherever there is a human being, there is an opportunity for a kindness."

— Seneca · 4 BC–65 AD

"The greatest gift is a portion of thyself."

— Ralph Waldo Emerson · 1803–1882

"Love is the joy of the good, the wonder of the wise, the amazement of the gods."

— Plato · 428–348 BC

"I would not wish any companion in the world but you."

— William Shakespeare · 1564–1616

"Without friends no one would choose to live, even if he had all other goods."

— Aristotle · 384–322 BC

"One of the most beautiful qualities of true friendship is to understand and to be understood."

— Seneca · 4 BC–65 AD

"A friend is one soul in two bodies."

— Aristotle · 384–322 BC

"Without feelings of respect, what is there to distinguish men from beasts?"

— Confucius · 551–479 BC

"Speak low, if you speak love."

— William Shakespeare · 1564–1616

"The strength of a nation derives from the integrity of the home."

— Confucius · 551–479 BC

"What injures the hive injures the bee."

— Marcus Aurelius · 121–180 AD

"It is one of the blessings of old friends that you can afford to be stupid with them."

— Ralph Waldo Emerson · 1803–1882

"Never impose on others what you would not choose for yourself."

— Confucius · 551–479 BC

"The only way to have a friend is to be one."

— Ralph Waldo Emerson · 1803–1882

"Lovers don't finally meet somewhere. They're in each other all along."

— Rumi · 1207–1273

"The course of true love never did run smooth."

— William Shakespeare · 1564–1616

VI · Wisdom & Self-Knowledge

Turn the lantern inward. The examined life shines outward from there.

"A man sees in the world what he carries in his heart."

— Johann Wolfgang von Goethe · 1749–1832

"Opinion is the medium between knowledge and ignorance."

— Plato · 428–348 BC

"Those who know do not speak. Those who speak do not know."

— Lao Tzu · 6th century BC

"Everything flows, nothing stands still."

— Heraclitus · 535–475 BC

"Not I, not anyone else can travel that road for you. You must travel it for yourself."

— Walt Whitman · 1819–1892

"Not till we have lost the world do we begin to find ourselves."

— Henry David Thoreau · 1817–1862

"The whole is more than the sum of its parts."

— Aristotle · 384–322 BC

"The greatest discovery of my generation is that a human being can alter his life by altering his attitudes."

— William James · 1842–1910

"The greatest thing in the world is to know how to belong to oneself."

— Michel de Montaigne · 1533–1592

"He who learns but does not think is lost. He who thinks but does not learn is in great danger."

— Confucius · 551–479 BC

"The first forty years of life give us the text; the next thirty supply the commentary."

— Arthur Schopenhauer · 1788–1860

"If the doors of perception were cleansed, everything would appear to man as it is: infinite."

— William Blake · 1757–1827

"Thinking is the talking of the soul with itself."

— Plato · 428–348 BC

"The heart has its reasons which reason knows nothing of."

— Blaise Pascal · 1623–1662

“*I exist as I am, that is enough.*”

— Walt Whitman · 1819–1892

“*I exist as I am, that is enough.*”

"Education is the kindling of a flame, not the filling of a vessel."

— Socrates · 470–399 BC

"Knowing yourself is the beginning of all wisdom."

— Aristotle · 384–322 BC

"Knowing yourself is the beginning of all wisdom."

"Real knowledge is to know the extent of one's ignorance."

— Confucius · 551–479 BC

"Life is really simple, but we insist on making it complicated."

— Confucius · 551–479 BC

"Ignorance is the root and stem of all evil."

— Plato · 428–348 BC

"Ignorance is the root and stem of all evil."

"Sell your cleverness and buy bewilderment."

— Rumi · 1207–1273

"Act without expectation."

— Lao Tzu · 6th century BC

"There is a candle in your heart, ready to be kindled."

— Rumi · 1207–1273

"There is a candle in your heart, ready to be kindled."

"Learning without thought is labor lost; thought without learning is perilous."

— Confucius · 551–479 BC

VII · Freedom, Simplicity & Not Keeping Score

The freest person is not the one who has the most, but the one who needs the least.

"I know the joy of fishes in the river through my own joy, as I go walking along the same river."

— Zhuangzi · 369–286 BC

"When you are content to be simply yourself and don't compare or compete, everyone will respect you."

— Lao Tzu · 6th century BC

"There is nothing either good or bad, but thinking makes it so."

— William Shakespeare · 1564–1616

"How vain it is to sit down to write when you have not stood up to live."

— Henry David Thoreau · 1817–1862

"To live is the rarest thing in the world. Most people exist, that is all."

— Oscar Wilde · 1854–1900

"He is richest who is content with the least, for contentment is the wealth of nature."

— Socrates · 470–399 BC

"Wealth is the ability to fully experience life."

— Henry David Thoreau · 1817–1862

"A man is rich in proportion to the number of things he can afford to let alone."

— Henry David Thoreau · 1817–1862

"It is enough to do good even if you do not receive credit for it."

— Marcus Aurelius · 121–180 AD

"Not all those who wander are lost."

— J.R.R. Tolkien · 1892–1973

"Silence is the sleep that nourishes wisdom."

— Francis Bacon · 1561–1626

"Silence is the sleep that nourishes wisdom."

"The things that matter most should never be at the mercy of the things that matter least."

— Johann Wolfgang von Goethe · 1749–1832

"You will not be punished for your anger; you will be punished by your anger."

— The Buddha · 563–483 BC

"Give me six hours to chop down a tree and I will spend the first four sharpening the axe."

— Abraham Lincoln · 1809–1865

"In the end, only three things matter: how much you loved, how gently you lived, and how gracefully you let go."

— The Buddha · 563–483 BC

"Every man I meet is my master in some point, and in that I learn of him."

— Ralph Waldo Emerson · 1803–1882

"Be yourself; everyone else is already taken."

— Oscar Wilde · 1854–1900

"If you seek tranquility, do less."

— Marcus Aurelius · 121–180 AD

"Health is the greatest possession. Contentment is the greatest treasure. Confidence is the greatest friend."

— Lao Tzu · 6th century BC

"It is in your power to withdraw yourself whenever you desire. Perfect tranquility within consists in the good ordering of the mind."

— Marcus Aurelius · 121–180 AD

"To do nothing is sometimes a good remedy."

*"Flow with whatever may happen, and let your mind be free.
Stay centered by accepting whatever you are doing."*

— Zhuangzi · 369–286 BC

"Men are disturbed not by things, but by the opinions about things."

— Epictetus · 50–135 AD

"I am not afraid of storms, for I am learning how to sail my ship."

— Louisa May Alcott · 1832–1888

"Our doubts are traitors, and make us lose the good we oft might win, by fearing to attempt."

— William Shakespeare · 1564–1616

"Beware of all enterprises that require new clothes."

— Henry David Thoreau · 1817–1862